Copyright 2018 *gloria jean Bodenmuller*

Editor *gloria jean Bodenmuller*

Front Cover *Siegfried and gloria jean Bodenmuller*

All rights reserved. No part of this book may be reproduced in any manner without prior written permission from the publisher.

ISBN-13: 978-1985882379

ISBN-10: 198588237X

The Master's Touch Publishing
www.christianbooks4children.com

Printed by CreateSpace

About the cover: *The bear is an original Steif Bear made in Germany. He was given to Siegfried when he was about two years old by Siegfried's beloved Mother (Mutti). As of this writing that makes the Bearly 79 years old.*

Siegfried remembers in his boyhood years during the bitter cold winter months of Germany, his dear Mother (Mutti) taught he and his brother how to knit. And knit they did, mostly making clothes, like the Bearly has on, for his endearing Bearly.

The beer stein brings memories of what Germany stood for; it's beer and the times Siegfried and his brother Walter, would hand carry a liter of beer from one of the many breweries in their hometown, to their Grandmother Bodenmuller, (Grossmutter Bodenmuller).

It is both Siegfried and my, hope and prayer, that ewe the reader will thoroughly enjoy *A Boy Named Siegfried.* And you will come to know and understand him and what it was like being born and raised during the war on your own country, from a child's perspective.

We also, want to thank our granddaughter; Laurel Shea

Bodenmuller for giving us the title of her Papa's memoirs, *A Boy Named Siegfried.*

As with all of “Our” books we give God the Father, Jesus the Son and the Holy Spirit, all Praise and glory!!!

We love hearing from ewe, please don't hesitate to write to us at;

gjbodenmuller@gmail.com

Proudly printed in; *The United States of America*

A man of few words, but our dad didn't have to say much to get my brother and I to straighten up and fly right! If we ever back-talked he or my mom all he had to do was look our way or worse, start coming our way and we would quickly change our tune!

Dad taught us to work hard and be responsible and to accept the consequences for our actions. Having his approval for a job well done was the most rewarding thing a boy could ask for. I'll cherish the countless hours dad spent with me in our barn fixing up my 1946 Ford.

Smoking cigars, drinking beer and having a bonfire are the things I'll look back on and smile!

Dad helped make me the man I am today and I strive to be like him in my adventures in fatherhood! Love you dad!

Franz Joseph Bodenmuller; Christian, husband of Jennifer, father of Steven, Kasey, Ryan and Hope, U.P.S. Driver, first son of Fred and gloria jean

Don't know where to begin.... my Dad is such a huge influence in my life! He's a real man, and has been through a lot in his life time! I love sitting with him over a beer and just listing to his stories of his past.

To have my Mom, who is a great writer, put my dad's life into a book of stories is great and I can't wait for others to read it! So, crack open a beer or whatever you like and enjoy!!

Jeffrey John Bodenmuller; Christian, husband of Lexie, father of Laurel and Aubrey, C.H.P. Officer, second son of Fred and gloria jean

The older I get the more I appreciate what is called "old school". I tend to gravitate to "old school " sights, sounds, values and people. Fred Bodenmuller is one of those people.

Over the years I have cherished the times we have shared. Hearing of his early life in Germany and his migration to where he is now. "Old school" values like honesty, integrity, loyalty, industry and faith in God are what I try to incorporate in my life and Fred is a fitting example.

May we hit many more golf balls together, eat many more cheeseburgers and spend more time on your porch enjoying each other and God!

Love ya man,
Pastor Bill Sidorvich

What papa means to me, well first off he is my grandpa and we have made so many amazing memories. I was going through my old photos and I found him and me playing in my sandbox. He also tells some of my favorite stories, when he first came to the United States. My favorite one is when he thought root beer was beer. I am so blessed to have a grandpa like him.

– Laurel Shea Bodenmuller

A red Cadillac with white leather seats, the smell of expensive cigars, rich aromatic pipe tobacco, and a bachelor apartment complete with a mini bar and beer dispenser. These were the first impressions I have as a boy of 10 or 11 years old of my future brother in law Fred Bodenmuller. That was 50 years ago and it was the first time I got to see a swinging bachelor complete with a 5-handicap golf game. Over the years I've witnessed this stern German transition to become the husband of my sister, father two wonderful boys who have become extraordinary family men themselves, hold down a career as a machinist, and develop a 20-acre ranch for his family. Somewhere along this journey Fred accepted Jesus as his savior and this decision has shaped his life even more. I look forward to reading his life story.
Bill Joseph
November 2017

Fred and I have been friends for over 45 years. We met in the 1970s when my wife Leslie and I moved to Redwood Estates, a small town in the Santa Cruz Mountains. Fred and his wife Gloria lived across the street.

I got to know him well. Our families spent Christmases, New Years, and most celebrations like the Fourth of July and Christmas together, often even walking as a foursome to neighbor's homes and celebrating with them.

Fred is a hard worker, always improving his property. In Redwood Estates, because weekends were his time, instead of sleeping in, he got up earlier to work even longer on his home.

Many weekends I'd come over and help him on his home improvement projects. I learned a lot about building, and his wife Gloria provided us with plenty of German beer, and German lunches.

For many years Fred made his own wine and beer, and sauerkraut, and I followed making my own beer and wine, but never as good as his. When they moved to the country, he started raising all his own food, from tomatoes, to beef and chicken.

Fred has a very sober personality, I never heard him tell a joke. Often he'll enjoy one of mine though.

He has always been a good friend, and I was surprised to find out a few years ago, that although he's 80- years old, he is on no medication, which he credits to healthy food and plenty of vitamins.

As you read his story, I think you'll find Fred is an interesting man, and his story of being born in Germany, working his way to Canada, then down to California is an exciting and inspiring one.

Hank Snyder, Christian Brother and Newsman

Introduction

This book has been a challenge over the last two years to compose; yet it has been a delight. Fred and i are very thankful to all who contributed to the completion of this book. We want to thank Joe and Karen Maddux in being not only faithful, caring, praying friend's, but also our cherished brother and sister-in-Christ.

Karen, for her love and preparing wonderful meals for us, as Joe helped work on our computer. At one time he put in more memory, got the computer up and running, saving us a large sum for the purchase of a new computer.

And now, as we work together to provide the final copy to the publisher, Joe is working diligently to get it done. What a blessing. Without his skill and expertise, i would be lost, i am ever so grateful.

Also, to Fred, for the many hours he spent with me, not only driving me an hour away for computer class, but sitting with me patiently as i worked on the manuscript with the computer tech.

Above all, we want to give thanks to God the Father, Christ, His Son and the Holy Spirit, for giving me the gift of putting pen to paper. Our prayer is this book will touch many hearts and lives, as we give Glory to God, PRAISE HIM!!!

i will close with Proverbs 17:17a; “A friend loves at all times...” That verse is to our dear brother and sister-in-Christ, Joe and Karen Maddux. THANK EWE!!!

We love ewe all and especially our Lord,
Fred and gloria jean Bodenmuller

Table of Contents

Chapter 1

The Story Goes On

It was a typical hot, humid summer in 1936, when she almost bled to death giving birth to her first born. He was a handsome son, with reddish hair like his paternal grandfather, which would be a hindrance, as he grew older. Having reddish hair was very rare for a boy, let alone brothers, growing up in war torn Germany. But it made them both strong and great defenders, which would pay off later in life. The war was just beginning on their Country, and they had to be tough. Then, at ages two and one, their father would be hospitalized for a year. He had been a gifted wood carver. Now Mom or Mutti, had to work during his hospitalization, in order to feed, clothe and house she and her small sons.

The treasured golden ring of his father still bears the initials of K. B. (Karl Bodenmuller) and the date Berta Schilling Bodenmuller placed it on his right ring finger, 1934. In Germany, the wedding ring is worn on the right ring finger, where as in America it is worn on the left.

They made their first home in Saulgau, Germany, his hometown. Herr Bodenmuller worked as a wood carver and Frau Bodenmuller was a homemaker, born and raised on a farm in Griessen, Germany. She later became an assistant to a midwife and housekeeper. Her husband was hospitalized for tuberculosis and a brain tumor. There was no cure for tuberculosis during that time. He eventually succumbed to the awful disease.

The first young son was named, Siegfried Franz Karl Bodenmuller and the second Walter Hugo Bodenmuller. Siegfried was three and Walter two years of age, at their father's death. Not long after his death, they and their mother moved in with their paternal grandparents, who also lived in Saulgau. Oma and Opa Bodenmuller had a two story home they rented; the upstairs would be the home for Berta and her two sons for a couple of years. Opa Bodenmuller was a Brewmeister (master brewer of beer). Siegfried remembers there were eleven breweries in Saulgau during that time. Oma Bodenmuller was a housewife (hausfrau), homemaker. They were married over fifty years when Opa died.

After his death, Berta, her two sons and Oma moved into another home in Saulgau. Oma lived with them for many years. Siegfried remembers Oma giving he and his brother a few "Pfinnig" or pennies to walk to one of the breweries and purchase a liter of beer for her to drink. They were just little tykes of ten and eleven years old. Carrying that liter of beer home was quite a feat; they stopped many a time, took a sip and walked on. By the time they reached home they consumed almost half of the liter of beer. Oma was pleased to have whatever was left.

Eventually, Berta (Mutti) was able to find work assisting a

mid-wife, which gave she and her son's opportunity to find an apartment to rent. Her son's were about three and four years old at the time. Not having a baby sitter and the need to work, she had to leave them in the apartment alone. Being so young, they got into many things before Mutti arrived home to prepare their lunch and then she would return to work. Siegfried remembers there was only one small window to look out, but it was so high up near the ceiling. He and his brother managed to stack boxes or whatever their little hands could handle, in order to just look out the window at the street below.

The baker lived next door and they could smell the fresh bread and baked goods permeate the air. Sometime later, the boys got their first dog. World War 2 broke out and they were starving and had very little heat in their tiny abode. Siegfried and his brother, Walter taught their beloved dog new tricks. One was to fetch the baker's briquettes so they could heat their home and cook on the cook stove.

As the war went on, work and food were in short supply Somehow; the Lord brought two Jewish men, a father and son to Mutti. She bravely took them into their home, knowing if she did, she and her son's could eat. They were able to bring food and supplies into their home. Which, Mutti and the boys were most thankful to get. Mutti had great faith in the Lord that He would provide for her and her two sons and yet protect them while these two Jewish men lived in their tiny apartment.

Siegfried's, Onkel Josef was very involved with the S.S. And had he had known Mutti had two Jewish men living with them, he would have had them all shot. Including, Siegfried his brother and Mutti. She was able to keep them hidden for quite some time during the war. Then one day the two Jewish men had to leave and defend their Country.

Siegfried remembers he and his brother stealing the farmer's chickens at night, while the farmer slept and the chickens roosted, in order to put food on their table. He also remembers his beloved childhood buddies being blown-up playing with ammunition and seeing so many dead lying on the streets of his small village, too numerous to count. He recalls the many times the children while attending school, were told to go into the bomb shelter for protection from the bombs. They also wore knickerbockers, which were good for filling up with stolen apples. They called them their apple stealing pants.

Not only did he feel the pain and loss of his father, but his aunt Fanny and two children who were killed during the war from a bomb attack. His aunt Ann was in the Luftwaffe (air force) and was also killed in the war, as well his uncle Hugo. All of them were relatives on his father's side.

Recently, we had a dear friend that was hospitalized, Fred and i visited. Upon leaving the hospital, Fred said, " This brings back memories for me going to the hospital in Germany visiting my father. My mother had to work to provide for us, so my brother and I would walk to the hospital to see our father. We were only allowed to visit him shortly, as he was in isolation due to having tuberculosis. And it was very frightened for us two boys, I was three and my brother was two. We spent most of the day at the hospital; baby sitters were unheard of at the time. The Catholic nuns provided most of the care with the patients and cared for us as well, by providing us with food until our mother arrived to take us home."

A couple years after the passing of their father, their mother was then hospitalized for a bleeding disorder. Probably, the same disorder she had when she gave birth to Siegfried. She remained in the hospital for a week or more. Siegfried says, "We were older then and could care for ourselves." i asked, "How old were you?" He replied, "Oh, we were in Kindergarten, about ages four and five." They would walk to the hospital visit with their mom and the nuns would feed them, then they would walk home to an empty house. The next day they did the same. This was during WW 2. One can only imagine. The boys grew up, fast and took on great responsibility. God was truly watching over them.

He and his brother Walter collected Luggers, pistols, guns, bullets, tank shells and other ammunition; they took from the dead soldiers. They hid their treasures in their cellar, knowing their dear Mother would not find them, because she did not like going into the dark cellar. As a result she did not know of all their lute until the war was over and the Mayor of their village had all the homes searched for hidden arsenal. What stinkers those two boys were, Mom indeed had her hands full. Bless her.

Although, Siegfried wishes he had some of those weapons today, as collector items to pass on to his two sons. Being so young he didn't understand the value of the weapons, let alone not being able to keep them.

Siegfried, his brother and buddies played with the ammo they had collected. Amazing. At one time they had a box of ammo sitting in a deliveryman's barn. The deliveryman made his rounds with horse and wagon. Once he had his wagon loaded and was off to make deliveries, the boys and their friends set off the box of ammo. The bullets went flying everywhere. Knocking out windows, putting holes in the barn and farmhouse. Did those boys ever get a lick-en when the delivery many arrived home.

On another occasion Siegfried, Walter and their buddies built a fire, dumped bullets they had found into the fire and bullets went flying everywhere for a good thirty minutes.

He and his brother found planes that had crashed in the forest near their home. And of course the two boys dismantled everything and anything they could take home. This was fascinating to them, they were so poor, and to have all this at their very fingertips was exciting.

At one time he and his brother were walking home from school and the planes began coming overhead dropping bombs. They quickly ran under a pear tree for shelter. Siegfried had been hit on the head, he thought for sure it was part of the effect of the bomb. Something dreadful was running down his face, he turned to his brother and cried out, "I've been shot!" His brother turned to him and began laughing, a fully ripe pear had fallen from the tree and hit Siegfried on the head and the juice was running down his face.

Chapter 2

How Does One Survive in War

The effects of the war hit his hometown of Saulgau, Germany in 1942, when Siegfried was a mere six years of age. The lights were turned off early and they sat in the dark or went to bed listening to the sound of the sirens or the bombs, filling the night air. When the bombs were dropped at night in Stuttgart, which was about one hundred miles away, he could see the whole sky light up from the distance. And hear the sound of the bombs being dropped. We can only imagine how frightening that must have been, especially for the children.

There were very few automobiles during those days, perhaps a motorcycle or the motorcycle with the sidecar. By the way, those are called, Schweiger Muter Toter. Translated that means Mother-in-law killer. Other than that, most drove around in horse and buggy, of course the train was for distant travel.

Siegfried was also in Hitler's Youth movement, where the young boys learned to carry wooden guns and march. Teaching them to fight the enemy. Each morning during the war he and his classmates were taught to say; Heil Hitler, yet didn't understand what it meant only seeing Hitler's picture hanging in every classroom. Like most Germans, they thought he was a wonderful man and were unaware of his cruelty, especially to the Jewish people.

As a young boy it seemed the war would never end, hearing the sirens going off, the bombs hitting their beloved land, the bloodshed, the violence, starvation for many, trying to keep their small abode warm in the long winter months and all the horror that comes with war. We in the United States for now can only read about the wars in our own country. We can hardly imagine day after day experiencing war on what seemed to be a never-ending battle.

During the war, Siegfried and his brother were able to have a small dog they taught to steel briquets from the nearby baker, the briquettes were used to help heat their small apartment. Sometimes the dog would not only bring several briquettes, he was coached to make his run for each one. The briquettes were used not only to heat their small home, but also to bake the bread Mutti made, when she was able to obtain flour. That wasn't too often, as flour and other staples were in short supply, as was the German Mark, for currency. Then at other times the pup brought a roll or two from the baker. Mmm, food at last and good too.

One time that little dog got Siegfried and his brother in big trouble. They decided to take this feisty little critter out for a walk, as they walked along with their pup they met up with the local butcher who happened to be riding his bike. The pup was fascinated with the wheels spinning on the bike, so attacked those moving tires while the butcher was on the bike peddling away. The dog knocked the butcher off his bike and nipped at his pant legs, tearing them. The butcher in his anger went after the dog and his owners, as they fervently tried to get the dogs paws out of the spokes of the bike. The dog in turn bit his owners. When they arrived home, they got another scolding from a much embarrassed mother. Yes, the war was tough, but "laughter is good medicine for the soul."

After almost four years to the day, September 2, 1945 the announcement came over the radio the war had ended. Siegfried remembers all the towns' people heading for the Bahnhof or railroad station to break in to it, knowing it was full of bread. Bread is a top staple for Germans. He also remembers finding banana peels left by the soldiers and scraping the inside of the skin for any piece of leftover banana. A fruit they knew nothing about prior to the war.

His aunt left he, his mom and brother 8,000 German Marks. They were so happy to receive some money, perhaps now things would be better.

They soon discovered the marks were worth nothing. As a matter of fact one could fill a wheelbarrow full of marks, which wouldn't even buy a pair of shoes, let alone a loaf of bread. The mark was absolutely worthless. If a person had a wheelbarrow full of marks and went into the market, leaving the wheelbarrow outside, someone would come along and take the wheelbarrow, which had more value than the money.

As for Siegfried's little village of Saulgau, the buildings were all bullet riddled from the war. The people walked around with terrified looks on their faces. So many had not only lost their homes but many of their family members and friends to the war. It would take many years to recover.

Chapter 3

A Feeling of Hope

Siegfried and his little family had not seen his maternal grandparents in almost four years. Personally, i have a difficult time just thinking about not seeing our grandchildren for such a length of time. We are so blessed.

When Siegfried, his mom and brother were able to take the train to visit his maternal grandparents, the train tracks were missing in many parts along the journey, due to the war and the bombs targeting the tracks. Many times they had to stay overnight at some filthy bug laden place until the tracks were repaired. Siegfried remembers those "wanson lagger" (bug stops) very well. Their bites left huge welts on their tender skin. Yet, they were so tired from the long journey, they were able to bring sleep to their worn bodies.

Once the tracks were repaired they would take their little belongings and walk quite a distance to get back on the train that would take them near Mutti's hometown of Griessen. The train did not stop in Griessen but in the neighboring town of Erzingen, which was much larger. From there she, Siegfried and Walter would walk with their suitcases the six or seven miles; sometimes it would be nightfall, before they reached Griessen.

In Griessen Mutti's big family, father, mother, aunts, uncles, and cousins would welcome them. This was Opa and Oma's Schilling, (although now passed) family farm where they would spend a couple of weeks. At last there they would enjoy good food, shelter and a loving family. And of course like most Germans, schafe, schafe, work, work. Much must be done on the farm. But Siegfried and Walter were happy to have a good meal for all their hard labor. Along with work, the boys would attend school, although the school they attended was on vacation. Education is very important in Germany. And of course church was a must every Sunday without fail, unless sick.

The chores before school were; feed and milk the cows, feed the hogs, the rabbits, and chickens before breakfast and then they walked to school. Upon arriving home the boys had homework and then field chores. Harvesting potatoes, taking the hay wagon out to collect the loose hay to put in the barn. The green hay was hand-cut with a scythe. The green grass was turned many times by hand until it was dry; it was not bailed. The Bodenmuller boys hitched the milk cows to the hay-wagon in order to harvest the hay. It was pitched with pitching forks to the high wagon. Then the boys jumped on top of the hay to tromp it down. Sometimes as they drove the hay-wagon to the barn, which was a couple of miles, part of the hay would fall off the wagon. They had to stop the wagon and pitch the hay back on the wagon. This chore sometimes took hours. Yet, once again it was all worth their effort, because a wonderful home-cooked meal was awaiting their hard work. The meal was farm fresh, sometimes pork for schnitzel, potatoes (kartoffel), carrots (gelberibba), and homemade bread from the big oven in the farm kitchen. Perhaps Linzer Torte for dessert and fresh milk from the cow to drink.

This part of Germany is known for potatoes, the area (Schwabenland) where Siegfried is from was known for Spatzle (homemade noodles). A tradition we carry on in our home and now our youngest son, Jeff, his wife Lexie and their two daughters will carry on.

During part of the war and after, Onkel Fritz and Tante Anna took over the farm. While the other Onkel's were serving in the war. Onkel Fritz served in the war as well and was captured and sent to Texas, United States of America.

Later on he would share stories about the good life he had as a P.O.W., in Texas. He had learned a lot about American farms and was excited to share with the family in Germany. Once being released and sent back home, much to his disappointment, he realized the work couldn't be done without the heavy farming equipment that was used in America. So it was back to the cows pulling the hay wagon and pitching the hay with pitchforks, harvesting the potatoes with aching backs and swiftly moving hands and all other farm work that had to be done without machinery.

All to soon it would be time for the Bodenmullers to make their trek to the train station and back to Saulgau. This time they would be laden not only with suitcases but good nourishing food. Mutti and her son's didn't mind; they knew they would eat well for a while, so the heavy load and distance was well worth the effort.

Once back in their hometown of Saulgau, the boys got a job herding and watching cows graze for a nearby farmer. After school each day they would walk miles from their hometown to their new job and adventure. Near the fields where the cows grazed was also a Catholic Convent. The Nuns would take their cows out to graze about the same time as the Bodenmuller boys. During one of those times Siegfried and Walter decided to venture into and visit the Nuns in the Convent. Siegfried remembers one of the Nuns sitting at a table painting delicate figurines. And wondered why she too didn't go out with the other Nuns watching the cows. As it turned out, the Nun was none other than **Sister Hummel, the famous painter of figurines**. The name of the Convent was Kloster Siessen.

In our future travels to Europe, i would see and really liked the Hummel figurines, yet they were too costly for our budget. During one of our visits a dear family friend gave me a picture by Sister Hummel of Mary holding baby Jesus. It is a treasure that hangs in our bedroom to this day. i often observe it, thanking the dear lady who gave it to me and think of the difficulties Mary faced in having and raising our Savior, Jesus. Also, i think of myself and other mother's in the honor and humbleness of giving us this great job of raising children, especially teaching them to worship the Lord and His word the Bible.

In the middle of the grazing land for the cows was the farmer's huge pile of leftover stems from the potato harvest. Siegfried and Walter would light a small pile to roast potatoes. Have ewe ever roasted potatoes in an outdoor fire? Without wrapping them in foil. They have a remarkable taste all their own. We did them in the “barn fires” bon fires that we would have on our ranch years later. Try it, with care sometime. You will be surprised.

Well, as boys will be boys, Siegfried and Walter were no different. Instead of lighting just a small pile of the potato stems, these two mischievous fellows decided to light the huge pile. The farmer's daughter was watching her parent’s cows and saw what they were doing; she immediately tried stomping out the flame. Much to her dismay, she could not keep up with two boys prank. Before long the whole pile was in flames. As for the boys, yes, they caught heck from the nearby farmer, it was endangering their home.

In the hot humid days of summer, when school was not in session, the Bodenmuller boys would walk to the nearby Zellersee (lake) for a swim. The lake was full of leeches, but this didn't bother the boys or the other children who swam in the lake. It was hot and humid; the water was refreshing.

As typical hard working German boys, not a moment was wasted. While at the lake, they would cut into the dryer parts of the lake, which gave them briquettes to use for firewood at home to keep their house warm in the winter. When the swimming was over, they hand carried their briquette treasures home. They were also good for Mutti to use as she cooked on a wood burning stove. I believe it is much like using dried cow pies for heat.

The last time we as a family visited Germany, as we were flying back home to California we met a passenger on the plane who was into archeology finds. He was telling Fred and i about his finds in Germany, particularly in a small lake. He went on naming the lake and the finds, which were in these briquettes they cut from the dryer part of the lake. Amazing historical things lie in these finds. After telling us all this information, i just looked at Fred; yes it was the same lake where he and his brother cut the dried parts for briquettes to heat their small abode. Life goes on.

Siegfried and Walter, much like my three sisters and i, shared one bicycle. They were so small and it was so big, they had to lean it against a wall in order to get on the seat. Mutti would also use the bicycle to take her two sons to school, which was a mile or so from home. She started them in school at the same time, since they were only fifteen months apart in age. One son would ride behind her and the other in front. Incredible, and she did it on a daily basis.

When the boys were younger they wore knicker bockers. Oh the many things those wonderful balloon shaped pants could hold. They would go to the lake and catch fish, at one time they let down the opening where the fish came through and abundance of fish swam past. Not fast enough, these two brothers were quick to grab them and put them in their knicker bockers, running and jumping as the fish swam around, until they reached home. What a meal Mutti would prepare with these fresh fish. On other occasions they would pick apples and load their pants so Mutti could bake Apfelstrudel. (Apple strudel). Other than the famous knicker bockers, Mutti would take some of their father's old suits and make clothes for her growing boys. She was a gifted, talented lady to make jackets, pants and whatever else was necessary for her little son's. i can just see her now first measuring those two rascals, without a pattern, cutting and shaping them to fit her boys. Then taking them to her old fashioned pedal Singer sewing machine and working away, putting on the final touches of buttons etc., by hand. Yes, she was an amazing lady.

Leder hosen was very popular in Germany, but Mutti could never afford them. The word Leder means leather and hosen is pants, leather pants. Yes, they are pants (shorts with suspenders) made out of very soft leather. They do not have a zipper, just a flap in front to unbutton for that God given purpose of relieving one's self. Siegfried inherited a pair from a long time German friend of ours not many years ago. They are so heavy, sturdy and will never wear out.

She also hand knitted socks for them and herself as well. i remember her bringing the wool yarn from Germany along with her knitting needles when she came to visit us in California. After her prayer time and Scripture reading, helping us on our ranch, mainly cleaning and sweeping almost every nook and cranny, (cleanliness of Germans), i learned a lot. Every day after lunch, Mutti would take a nap, after her nap she took out her knitting and made those wonderful warm socks for Siegfried, Franz, Jeffrey and i.

Later on the Siegfried and Walter acquired an aquarium from a friend who had built it. This was such a joy and entertainment for these two young men who had very little. One thing for sure, coming from such dire poverty, they appreciated and cared for everything, and still do today as well.

In order to help with adding income to their home, the Bodenmuller boys worked at a bowling alley. Not like your typical alley today, where everything is automation. They were there to set-up the bowling pins as the men played. What a chore, i would soon forget where to place each pen after each play. The pins were made out of wood and they would fly all over as the men struck them with the ball, making it dangerous for the boys to retrieve the pens. But they did it with zeal, knowing this would help put food on their table. By the way, the game was only for the wealthy in those days.

On one of their visits to the family farm in Weisweil they visited an Onkel (Uncle) who raised not only rabbits but also small dogs. While visiting the Onkel gave them toothbrushes and told the boys to go and brush the rabbits teeth. Little did they know that it wasn't necessary to brush a rabbits teeth, but being obedient to his wishes they tried desperately to brush the rabbits teeth, with not much success.

Prior to their departure the Onkel gave them one of his pups. It was a female; the boys didn't want a female so they switched for a male without the Onkel knowing. The boys would pay for their trickery. The pup became a feisty critter, as it grew older. That is the very dog i mentioned earlier who went after the butcher while he was riding his bicycle. It doesn't pay to be dishonest, a lesson we must all learn.

School days were not easy for Siegfried as he had difficulty staying focused. Mmm, sounds familiar, with his son as well. At one point during his early years of school, he had an Aunt as his teacher. She was constantly reprimanding Siegfried and Walter. Then one day it happened, the moment she had her back to the students, he and Walter climbed out the classroom window and off they went to play. When they finally decided to return home, Mutti was waiting with the stick to discipline them. Word got out so fast, even without a phone. They were in school the next day.

The education system is much different than in America. School age begins at five with Kindergarten. (The German word we later adopted, "children's garden"). At age twelve the student attends Gymnasuim, which is the equivalent to beginning year of High School (younger age). At age fifteen the student either attends a trade school or goes on to college and a profession.

Chapter 4

Finally an Opportunity to work in His Trade

Siegfried went on to trade school, which takes three years to complete a chosen trade. He served as an apprentice as a tool and die maker at a company called Bautz where his Onkle Josef Bodenmuller worked. Although, being a tool and die maker was not Siegfried's choice he said, “Because my Onkle was a tool and die maker, he told me that's what I would become as well.” During his time as an apprentice he earned a small income and gave it to Mutti to run the household, keeping a smaller amount for himself.

Siegfried's mode of travel back and forth to trade school/work was a bicycle. He put the bicycle together with parts he found from the city dump. When the harsh Winters of Germany came, he had difficulty riding the bike to and from work, so walked in the freezing cold. Giving thanks for every step, having a job and income to help support his family. On one occasion as he was riding his bike to work he stopped at the railroad crossing. In those days there was a man in a booth who let the bars down to stop the traffic for the on coming train. That particular icy morning, Siegfried slid into the bars coming to an immediate halt. At that moment the man in the booth lifted the bars to allow the traffic to pass, as he did, up went Siegfried's bike stuck in the bars. He had to walk up to the booth/tower to tell the man to let the bars down so he could retrieve his precious mode of travel, his bike. On a different occasion, as he waited for the train to pass one of the passengers threw Siegfried an apple from the moving train, as a kind gesture. Well, it wasn't to be, it hit him straight on the forehead almost knocking him out.

Prior to having a good job at Bautz, Siegfried loved the idea of skiing so decided to make his own pair of skis. In doing so, he took two wine barrel slats and with ropes tied them onto his shoes, sticks for poles, climbed to the top of a snowy hill and off he went. He enjoyed the thrill of going down that hill so much, he saved from his earnings at Bautz (after giving Mutti most of what he earned) for a pair of real skis and poles and of course warm clothing

Siegfried and his brother Walter also decided to take-up photography and not just taking pictures, but learning to mix the chemicals and developing them in their makeshift dark room.

These young men got so good at taking and developing pictures, many were asking them to take pictures for them and before long they had a business. They even won prizes for some of the photos they took and developed. This too would be profitable later on.

During the winter, once a year, for one week Bautz would

offer their lodge for its employee's in the Bavarian Alps. The lodge was at the bottom of the Alps. If an employee wanted to go to the lodge at the top of the mountain, he had to hike up the snowy cliffs and then ski down. Of course Siegfried was at the top of the list to go on the four-hour hike up the mountain to the top where the lodge was awaiting with a nice warm fire, hot food and plenty of beer or wine. The trek would begin after a hearty breakfast; ski lifts were unheard of in those days. Thirty young and old energetic people would side step with their skis strapped onto their shoes up the steep mountain to reach the lodge. After eating a hearty meal and some rest, the trip now on skis would begin, which took one and one half hours. Many times they would not reach the bottom until nightfall. Siegfried was the brave one who skied with a flashlight in his mouth, as he led the brave pack down the mountain surrounded by the darkness. As the other skiers followed the flashlight laden young man, Siegfried, if he fell, they all piled on top of him. He was careful not to hit a tree or any danger in their path.

It was during this time that he and his brother's photography came into use. Many of the skiers did not even own a camera and were delighted to pay the brothers to take and develop pictures of this fun event. Oh my, entrepreneurs at an early age.

Siegfried took great interest in flying and the Graff Zeppelin, named after Count Ferdinand von Zeppelin, fascinated him when it flew overhead when he was a young boy. That history, he learned and had no idea what it meant at the time. Flight was still new and exciting.

At the age of fifteen he helped his Onkel George in Griessen build a sailplane, which was made of balsa wood. Many a time they would load it on the top of the hay wagon and haul it out to a hilltop in Griessen. Siegfried being the brave rambunctious person he is, quickly got into the cockpit of the plane. Although, feeling frightened yet excited sailed into the blue-clouded skies of Germany. Soon after, Onkel George decided not to keep the plane as it took a lot of time to mend each time it crashed on the hard ground of the green meadows of German soil.

At an early age during the cold winter months, Mutti would send her son's out in the snow barefoot, just before bedtime. She would stay indoors with the doors locked as she peered out the window watching her boys run fast through the icy cold snow. This wasn't punishment by any means; Mutti had a plan.

They were only out a few minutes, just long enough to get their feet warm and blood circulating before they dove into their warm feather comforters for bedtime. Usually, the fire from the coal-burning stove that heated their tiny apartment went out during the night and they got up to a very freezing cold house. The walls on most of the old buildings in Germany are made of cement, which is about three to four feet in width. Cement does not keep in the heat. Siegfried remembers in those cold mornings as he awakened, the walls next to his bed had ice on them; now that is cold.

Wood was used to kindle the fire and then the briquettes of coal were added. The firewood was collected during the summer and fall months. Siegfried, Walter and Mutti would take hand pulled wagon with wooden sides, out to the forest, cut and gather wood. This was an all day chore. The wood first had to be gathered from fallen trees or limbs, then cut with a handsaw or chopped with an axe into small pieces in order to fit in the small wagon and firebox for the stove. Once the wagonload was full, they pulled it home, dumped it and went for more wood. Within the next several days, they would then take the wood and stack it, carrying it in baskets up a couple flights of stairs to the attic. Why the attic and not outdoors? Because the attic was warm and kept the wood dry for winter. Stacking it outdoors, was unheard of, due to the cold snowy Winters and no way to cover the wood, as we have plastic today. There is also a special German technique, Siegfried has taught me in wood stacking. It works well, without having the whole pile of wood on top of you, when you retrieve wood for the fire. Nonetheless, whether it fell on you or not, the wood for starting the fire in the winter had to be retrieved up that long flight of stairs that led to the attic.

While working at Bautz as an apprentice, Siegfried's Onkel Joseph treated him fairly. More so than he did when he and his brother worked for him on he and his Tante's home. After his Tante died, Onkel Joseph showed great interest in Mutti, the feeling wasn't mutual and the boys did not care for him as a father image either.

Sometime later he met Tante Josephine (Fine) and they

would soon marry. Together they built a small home in Saulgau, which Siegfried and Walter helped build, for food. Siegfried stated, "he did not like me as much as he liked my brother." Not many got along with this harsh, grumpy, unhappy man. He didn't attend church, yet he sang with the church choir, because he had a good voice. Yet, he wanted nothing to do with God or the church. Tante Fine, on the other hand was just the opposite with her loving, kind, generous spirit.

Chapter 5

That Burning Desire

Siegfried's desire was to go to America one day, to make the United States of America his home. He saved his German Marks several times for the flight and other needs. Actually, his goal was to go to South America and see the great Amazon River. He had heard so much about America while attending school and loved what the American flag and America stood for; freedom. He didn't like the culture of the different class's in Europe, white collar and blue-collar workers. He felt everyone should be treated equally and with respect, no matter his or her position. Not because if you had a degree you should be treated with more respect than one without one. As much as he loved Mutti, he was walking away from her faith that he thought was crammed into him. Although, Mutti lived her faith, read the Bible to her son's and prayed with them, he just couldn't accept it. He wanted to get away from that as well, and just kept thinking about going to America.

The many times he had saved to make the trip to America, he spent the money on different things he wanted, one being a B.M.W. Motorcycle. He recalls, "It was so big and I weighed about one hundred and ten pounds and was afraid to ride it.

The only time I got the courage to ride it, was getting drunk and then I hit the rode on my B.M.W. Motorcycle." Crazy, not only endangering his life but the lives of others. He went on, "Finally, I sold it and began saving again, believing this time I was really going to make the journey I had so desired in my heart."

At age fifteen or sixteen Siegfried and Walter, and several buddies decided to take a dance course that was offered in a studio in Saulgau. The course lasted at least six months, with practice twice a week. They would pay for the lessons with the little they had left over they earned from work. They learned the Tango, Waltz, Fox Trot, Rumba and Cha, Cha, Cha.

This was quite an ordeal for these young Germans who only knew the Polka and other German dances. The group included twelve to fifteen couples. At the end of the course they had a performance for anyone who cared to watch. It was after their performance they would receive their certification, if so earned. Siegfried and Walter did well, and received their desired certification. Years later when Siegfried was competing in a dance Marathon while residing in Canada, this course would pay-off. Although, in the Marathon they danced to the new Rock and Roll beat as well, which at times, being so tired caught he and his partner off-guard. The prize for that event was twenty-five Canadian dollars, which was a great deal, when Siegfried was only earning fifty cents an hour. After twelve hours his partner walked off the dance floor, she was not able to dance one more step. This disqualified Siegfried (who was still going strong) as well.

Dance is still one of the activities he and gloria jean still enjoy today. Both have a love for music and enjoy expressing that gift with dance. As a matter of fact that is exactly where they first met on the dance floor. Another story, for later.

Chapter 6

A Desire Fulfilled

Time to celebrate, Siegfried had finally done it again, he'd saved to make the trip to America or at least Canada. All of his buddies, gal friends and his brother gathered for the fun event leading to his departure. The German beer and wine flowed, with the new American rock and roll music and dance. His suitcase was packed, to the limit of fifty pounds. In the morning he would don his heavy and I do mean heavy winter coat, packed with sausage, cheese, drinks and sandwiches made by Mutti for the long trip. No meals were served aboard those planes in those days and there were no bathroom facilities.

As he went to his family to say his final aufwiedersehen, he told his aging (ninety-five year old) Oma Bodenmuller he was going to Stuttgart, in order not to alarm her. She knew better, when she said, "You are going to America. And I want you to promise you will recite the Lord's Prayer, every day before you get out of bed. He agreed and has kept that promise these many years later. He said it in German then, now says it in both German and English every morning before arising.

The year was 1956 when he boarded the plane from

Stuttgart to Frankfurt and on to New Foundlen. The flight would take ten to twelve hours before it landed in Gander. He remembers the plane flew so low to the ground and the ocean; it was as though one could reach their hand out and actually touch the water. He could see the fire coming out of the engines as it flew over the Atlantic Ocean. There were no jets in those days.

Finally, it landed in Gander, and there was ice and snow on the runway as the plane skid and came to a halt, landing on its side. The side it landed on was opposite the exit door, making it difficult to get off the plane. He remembers women, children and people screaming in fear as they landed. Once off the plane, they had a layover all night at the airport, awaiting the new plane that would take them to Toronto, Canada.

At long last the plane arrived and took the tired, forlorn, passengers to Toronto. The month was April and winter had set-in with icy cold snow on the ground. What was Siegfried thinking coming to Canada for a warmer climate than Germany? Mmmm, wonder if he knew his geography. His friend Walter from Germany made the flight with him, because he had connections in the United States, which would be their next adventure. A family in Germany had relatives in Toronto who picked them up at the airport and took them directly to a Hungarian family's home, where they would have room and board and get out of the cold. Only one major problem faced these young immigrants. Neither one of them spoke English.

The very next day after a hearty breakfast, Siegfried walked the streets of Toronto in search of work, any kind of work, just to pay his room and board for the time being. He walked into a bakery and was hired at fifty cents an hour. In Germany he was making four to five dollars an hour in his trade as a tool and die maker. He worked in the bakery for a month, while still looking for a job in his learned trade.

The day finally came when he would be employed by Toronto Machine Repair. It was owned and operated by a Russian man and his wife. To Siegfried's gratefulness, the foreman was German. The owner spoke very little German, and took this young German immigrant into his and his wife's life. They had no children and immediately took a liking to Siegfried. They owned a farm outside of the big city of Toronto, and on weekends invited Siegfried to spend time helping on the farm. Much to his delight, he welcomed the invitation as he loved the outdoors, the fresh country air and the work was a pleasure after being in the machine shop all week long. Besides, it reminded him of his grandparents' farm in Germany. The farm was located near Lake Ontario.

One fine day as Siegfried went to the garden shed on the farm to retrieve a shovel, he stopped in his tracks; there in the shed was what he thought a friendly black and white cat. As he went to pet the critter, the old farmer called out in German, "Halt."(Stop) Too late, a pungent spray filled the air, most of it on Siegfried. Much to his surprise and for the first time in his life he had an encounter with a skunk. A critter he had read about in Germany, but had never seen, because they do not have them in Germany. Quickly, the farmer and his wife gave Siegfried an unwelcome bath in tomato juice to help get rid of the smell.

As I mentioned before, Siegfried and his friend, Walter did not speak English. During the night in their shared room, Walter would get up and sleep walk. While doing so, he spoke perfect English. The next day when Siegfried would tell him what he had done, he had no idea and couldn't speak a word of English while awake. Another ordeal these two beer drinking German young men met was no beer or alcohol could be purchased from Friday through Sunday in Canada. So they, like many others would stock-up on Thursday. So much for control.

When Siegfried first arrived in Canada and went to a restaurant to eat he was given a glass of water prior to ordering. This is unheard of in Europe, he thought, maybe they want me to wash my hands first, so that is exactly what he did and used the lovely convenient cloth napkin to dry them. Not being able to read English, let alone speak it, he noticed root beer was on the menu. Hmmm, he thought this must be beer. With that he ordered root beer, after tasting it, he thought, 'They sure don't know how to make beer.'

Chapter 7

The Great Adventure

Canada Seems More Like Home

The great adventure: After living in Toronto for a year or so, Siegfried made friends with several young men his age. They decided to go on a hunting trip. The trip would be to El Con, Alaska, camping out in the wilderness for two to three days. They would fly across Canada to Alaska in a small aircraft, which would drop them off somewhere in the middle of nowhere. Of course they would have packed plenty of food in ice chests, along with all their warm camping gear.

It was a long trip in that small aircraft, flying over the expanse of Canada. Somehow the expert pilot was able to land the aircraft in that dense wilderness. Once the tents were pitched and they got ready for bed, they heard loud noises in the camp. Peering through the opening in the tent they spotted not one but several bears going through all their supplies Too frightened to leave the tent, they decided to let the bears have a feast and clean-up when daylight broke, to the mess the bears had left.

After scrounging around for what little food was left for breakfast, the men decided it was time to load their guns and a hunting we will go. The cost of the hunting trip was a week's wages, which was not cheap. They needed to make their trip worthwhile. As they walked through the wilderness one of them saw a moose and without hesitation shot it. Sad to say, he only wounded the massive critter. The moose was so angry from the wound and went after the first person it saw, Siegfried. Quickly, Siegfried was up a spindly tree as the moose butted his head into the trunk, all the while digging in the dirt and scraping the tree. One frightened young man hung on for dear life, as the moose continued his rampage.

This brought back memories for Siegfried when he and his brother were playing in the German forest as youngsters and a wild boar came after Siegfried. He had found a sturdy tree to climb, at that time. The boar dug and banged into the tree until nightfall and finally gave-up, running off into the forest. Siegfried and his brother went running home. This time, the moose wasn't about to give-up and the little tree was giving way. Finally, Siegfried's buddy aimed, fired and killed the giant moose. They proceeded to cut-up the meat and pack as much as they could in the ice chests for their long trip home. They were only able to pack half of the meat; the rest was left for the critters in the wild. After a few days, they were thankful to see a plane fly in and take these tough hunters home. Siegfried decided it was easier to purchase the meat at the market and that was the end of hunting for him.

He was beginning to like his new home in Canada and put off going to the United States of America. With that in mind he traveled just over the Canadian border into Wisconsin and fell in love with the land. It reminded him of Germany. He was surprised that he could purchase the American soil without being a resident; that was unheard of in Germany. So he decided to purchase the forty acres near Iron Mountain, Wisconsin. There were twenty acres of timber and twenty acres of open grazing land. The purchase was a mere four hundred and fifty dollars. It was gorgeous in the spring, summer and fall, but too much snow and hard winters, too much like Germany, that deterred him from staying on the land.

As for the Russian man, Siegfried worked for in Toronto, he and his wife did not want their now almost adopted German son to leave for America. As a matter of fact, they owned about a block in Toronto where the machine shop sat and he and his wife encouraged Siegfried to stay and he would have probably inherited the property, because they had no children.

Years later, while working in Mountain View, California where Siegfried was a foreman of a machine shop, he had a young man from Switzerland who was under his employ. The young Swiss had just come into California after working in Toronto, Canada. He went on to tell Siegfried the property where the Russian man and his wife owned was worth a fortune, as it was in the heart of Toronto. Guess it was not the Lord's plan for Siegfried to stay in Canada.

While in Canada Siegfried and his buddies decided they would go to one of the great lakes and get a nice suntan, since the weather was hot and humid. As they lay on the beach next to the beautiful lake, the sun shone brightly on their tender white German skin.

They were in and out of the cool water most of the day; sunscreen was unheard of in those days. But we did have wonder of wonders baby oil, oh my. By the time it got dusk and they were ready to head home, they could barely sit on the seat of the car from the pain of the sunburn. Once home, they looked in the mirror and low and behold every part of their bodies was a lobster red, with the exception of where their swimming trunks were. This experience they did not want to repeat again, but Siegfried did once again when he got to the United States, years later. How we soon forget.

Siegfried needed a car, not only for work but to get around in the big city of Toronto. He went to the department of motor vehicles and took the drivers test twice, before passing. The car was a 1948 or 1949 Chevy that was so beat up from the salt that was put on the roadways, due to the snow. The underneath of the car was all rotted out, similar to a Flintstone. With his old junk of a car he taught his landlord how to drive and his landlord went with Fred (and Fred's delightful German accent, that he still has) when he took his driver's test. It was a good idea that Siegfried taught him how to drive. Later the landlord would be the one to take Siegfried to the bus station to the bus that would take him to the United States of America. Siegfried remembers driving his old clunk around Toronto and many times getting lost.

Chapter 8

It's Time to say Aufweidersehen, Again

The year was 1959 and Siegfried finally made the decision to apply for a visa to go to the United States of America. One reason was he was tired of the cold hard winters, which were much like Germany. At that time he needed a sponsor to be able to enter the U.S.A. And the sponsor had to put up $8,000.00 U.S. dollars, if the immigrant failed to live up to his commitment, he would be deported to his homeland and the sponsor would loose the $8,000.00 dollars. That was like coming up with $50,000.00 or more in today's market. Who would sponsor this young German immigrant and his friend Walter? It was Walter's uncle who would put up the money, he owned a furniture store in New Jersey and was willing to sponsor the two young men. What a blessing. The Russian man and wife were very disappointed in Siegfried's decision to leave. They were in great hopes he would take over the machine shop business. Much to their dismay, the young adventurous German had made up his mind and there was no turning back. He was going to fulfill his dream of going to the United States of America.

Siegfried bought his one-way ticket with Greyhound from Canada to San Francisco, California for $120.00. His landlord dropped him off at the bus station and Siegfried was on his way to see the Country he had always dreamed about. As yet, he still could not speak English, daring, I would say so, or crazy. His first thoughts of seeing the United States of America from the bus's window were; 'It is so big and wide open country' He traveled through Michigan, Chicago, Laramie, and so on, purchasing picture post cards along the way. He would later place them all in an album and send it to his dear Mutti in Germany.

The bus would stop in many places along the way, Siegfried would have opportunities to see a rodeo in Laramie, Wyoming, gamble in Las Vegas and do and see other things he only dreamed of while in Germany. This was quite an adventure that would take a month. He also, looked for jobs along the way, learned to exchange Canadian dollars for American dollars. He found the people were very friendly and helpful. And he was not fearful of making the trip.

Finally, he had arrived. It was about four or five in the afternoon when the bus pulled into it's and Siegfried's final destination, San Francisco, California. The very first thing he did was purchasing a newspaper to look for a room to rent. In it, he found one on Oak and Steiner for fifty dollars a month for one room. He was paying fourteen for room and board in Canada and knew his next move was to find a job. The very next day he went to a phone booth and diligently searched for work, preferably at a large company. Without a car he began walking the streets of San Francisco to familiarize himself with the big city and to continue looking for work. Each day he walked and walked throughout the city, many times getting lost. (Which is one of his traits).

His supply of food was running out and he really needed a job. One day his landlord came in with a nice pigeon and told Siegfried to open his window and let it out. Siegfried remembered the days in W.W.2 as a young boy and wondering where their next meal would be. He couldn't let this happen again. This pigeon looked mighty good and it was. It was a God sent pigeon, i believe. He met a neighbor who told him about a job at an elevator company, near the waterfront. Siegfried hopped on a streetcar and landed his first job; he learned how to cut metal and was thankful to have a job that paid $2.25 an hour.

He saved his money and was able to purchase a used car, of course, with a stick shift. The total cost was $300.00 for the '55 Chevy four door. Gas was twenty-five cents a gallon. He had to learn not only to drive that stick shift in hilly San Francisco, but also to park it so it wouldn't roll down the hill and end up who knows where. After getting lost so many times, he decided to finally buy a map of the big city.

Not long after he found another job working for Schlagelock, where he could finally use his trade as a tool and die maker. Many of the men who worked there, were also German and spoke it as well. Siegfried felt more at home in his trade and being around his native tongue.

While living in the room, he met the neighbors who

invited him to dinner. For the first time Siegfried was introduced to greens, grits hog jowl and other types of Southern food, he ate it all, even the corn on the cob, which was only fed to the pigs in Germany. The neighbor who invited him was African American and was stationed in Germany at one time, and was delighted to help this young German immigrant.

During those days, when Siegfried walked the streets of San Francisco, he came across the Rothskeller, a German restaurant. It was there he met his long time friend Heinrich (Henry). Henry had a car and he took Siegfried around the city and many places. He also introduced him to a German family the Kranzs. They both enjoyed going there for an authentic German meal.

Henry sent for a mail order bride, Heidi, who was from Germany. They decided they would go to Reno to be married and Siegfried would be their best man. Once there and during the ceremony, Siegfried was asked for the ring. He searched and searched his jacket pocket, but couldn't find the ring. Panicked, he kept searching and soon found he had a hole in his pocket that the ring had slipped through. Today, both men laugh about the lost ring. And remark, "Maybe it shouldn't have been discovered" because their marriage ended in a terrible divorce.

Henry introduced Siegfried to another German, Armin. This was a blessing; because Siegfried was laid off at Schlaglock and Armin invited him to move in with him down the peninsula, Menlo Park to be exact. Today, Menlo Park is one of the most sought out expensive places to live in California or perhaps the United States. While living in Menlo Park, Siegfried started work for Cook Research Labs, where he would work for a couple of years as a machinist.

While living in an apartment, Siegfried and Armin purchased a television, probably the first either one owned. They decided to paint the wood on the television, black and began spray painting. Once they lifted the television to it's proper place, they noticed the carpet had a different tinge where the television sat. So, they decided to spray paint that area to match the rest of the carpet.

Neither, Armin or Siegfried were good cooks, but they ate well in spite of it. When they went to the market to purchase food, they would come home with several brown paper grocery bags, full of groceries for a mere twenty dollars or so. That was living.

While working at Cook's Research, Siegfried met Michael Dulkevich, who had difficulty-pronouncing Siegfried and soon changed his name to Fred. That began a new life for Siegfried having an American name, Fred. Michael or Mike had a home in Santa Clara in which he rented rooms. He asked Fred if he would like to rent a room from him.

The year was 1962 and Country and Western music was popular. A very small man also rented a room from Mike; his name was Little Jimmy Dickens. Yes, the same Country Hall of Famer. During those days living with Fred and Mike, Jimmy would bring out his guitar, sing and play. Fred would hear him and think, he is howling and told him, "Why don't you give it up, you will never amount to anything." Ooops.

While living in Santa Clara, the guys would attend Naberdack Hall to hear the Country and Western singers of the day. Johnny Cash was one of the performers, yet he was just beginning his career. There were many others who would in later years become hits. Fred was really becoming Americanized as he enjoyed going to the Hall and hearing these performers.

Fred's birthday came and he decided to make a Linzer Torte. It has spicy hard dough with a jam filling and is very popular in Germany. Well, his came out so hard that if the guys threw it, and it hit you just right, it would have knocked you out cold. That was Fred's last try at baking.

Fred and Mike each owned the American dream car, a Cadillac. Fred's was a 1954 yellow Coupe de Ville, Mike had a blue one just like it. Mike hooked both cars up with C. B.'s so they could communicate where the girls were, as they drove around the bay area. Mike and Jimmy were both divorced and Fred was single. Fred remembers the beautiful orchards that surrounded the now tract homes throughout Santa Clara and Santa Clara Valley/Silicon Valley.

During this time Fred met his first wife, who had a son and they had a daughter together, they named Heidi. Their marriage only last five or so years. Fred went back to Germany for the first time since he had left to visit family and friends. On his return trip his wife wanted a divorce. He granted her wish and continued to support their daughter for many years.

Chapter 9

A New Beginning and True Love

One stormy rainy night in February Fred met a young, green eyed, vivacious blonde; gloria jean Joseph at Loser's North, a disco in San Jose. They slowed danced to the hit tune of the day by the songbird; Frank Sinatra; **Strangers In The Night.** Fifty some years later, that is still their song and they are still singing and dancing along with the cruiser, as they both love to dance and still do to this very day. As Fred (Siegfried) and gloria jean agree and the rest is history. HIS STORY.

Actually, you may read the rest of the story in, The Girl From Silicon Valley. (If you haven't already.)

Aufweidershen und Gottes Segen

I'll be seeing you and God's Blessings.

Conclusion

Well, here i am concluding my husband Siegfried's story. i admit it wasn't as easy to write as my story, reason being it is not my story and he, as many of you know, is a very quiet man, keeping most things to himself. So why did i even attempt to write 'his story'? First, i wanted our children and grandchildren to know more about him and his life and secondly, many have come to me, after i wrote my story, asking when i was going to write, Siegfried's or Fred's?

So here it is after two years of compiling information, pictures and other details. Believe me, it was a challenge. After i had completed 'his story', he has shared many things he experienced over his lifetime of these eighty-one years. i think i should add them, but have decided what is written is written.

With that in mind, i believe you, the reader, will enjoy what has been written on paper. Hopefully, it will bring more insight to those who know or do not know Siegfried, what it was like growing up in the midst of the horrors and blessings of W.W. 2 in Germany. Blessings, we think, how can there be any blessing in war. Yet with God, He provides in ways that are beyond our imagination.

The story goes on to tell of his dream of coming to Canada and then on to the United States of America. Where his story ends, mine begins, The Girl From Silicon Valley. Where mine ends, his story begins. So, if you haven't purchased a copy of; The Girl From Silicon Valley, may i encourage you to do so, and then Siegfried's story will be complete.

Siegfried and i now reside in the small town in California, of Valley Springs. We really like our new abode and most of the conveniences are close, which is important, as one ages. We attend a wonderful Cowboy Church called; Glory Bound Fellowship, and believe me there is a lot of good old-fashioned fellowship, and barnyard theology from our wonderful Pastors. We have made some marvelous new silver, friends and keep the golden one's close to our hearts.

Our oldest son, Franz, and his wife, Jennifer, and their four children, live an hour away. The Lord directed me to live close enough to be there for them, yet not in their backyard. Our second son Jeffrey and his wife, Lexie, and their two daughters live about a three-hour drive away. We love and miss them all.

In closing as with my 'story' Johann Sebastian Bach, who began his work by writing “JJ---Jesu, “Jesus, help me”--- on his manuscript. That is the universal prayer for all writers. At the end of a piece he would write three letters---- S.D.G. Or Soli Deo gloria, which means “To the glory of God.”

My prayer is that this work will be a blessing to each and everyone who reads it and may God the Father, Christ the Son and the Holy Spirit receive the glory!!!

Aufweidersehen, gloria jean Bodenmuller

Herr und Frau Karl Bodenmuller, on their wedding day.

Siegfried at an early age, pretend smoking a pipe

Walter on left, Siegfried on right.

Siegfried’s hometown of Saulgau, Germany

Walter on the left, Siegfried on the right.

Mutti, Opa and Oma Bodenmuller, Walter and Siegfried.

Siegfried and partner, dance course.

„Was der Mensch sät;
wird er auch ernten!“

Graduation for Siegfried. The Bible verse;
“What so ever a man sows, that he also reaps.”
Galatians 6:7.

Siegfried skiing in the Austrian Alps
Without lifts, walked up the slopes and skied down.

Siegfried skiing with his buddies, in the Alps.

Onkle Georg's sailplane, Siegfried flew.

Siegfried's first car, while living in Canada

Toronto Canada, 1956. Siegfried's home for three years.

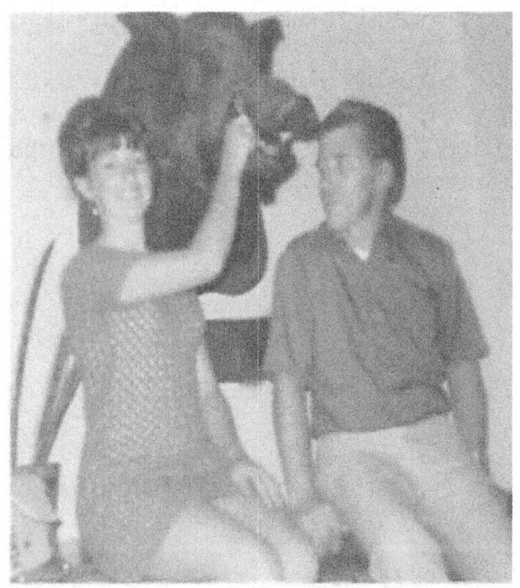

Gloria Jean Joseph, the love of Siegfried's life. Not the boar.

Siegfried's dream car, a Mercedes-Benz.
Purchased at the factory in Germany

Our son's Franz and Jeffrey, standing in front of the Schilling farmhouse in Germany.
Siegfried's Grandparents home.

Siegfried, Franz and Jeffrey in front of Siegfried's school in Saulgau, Germany.

Walter on the left, Siegfried on the right.
True German's, enjoying their beer.

Oma Bodenmuller (Mutti) visits us in America.
Siegfried, Jeffrey, Franz and Oma.

Family Photo

Siegfried (Fred), Franz and gloria jean

Fred, Jeff and I

All of our family

Our Wedding, April 20, 1968

Our 25th Wedding Anniversary

Our Golden Wedding Anniversary 2018

Saulgau, den 22. Juli 1950.

Mein Lebenslauf:

Ich bin am 28. Juli 1936 als Sohn des Bild=
hauers Karl Bodenmüller und der Berta
Bodenmüller geb. Schilling in Saulgau ge=
boren. Ich bin jetzt 14 Jahre alt und werde
nächstes Jahr aus der kath. Volkschule mit
meinem ein Jahr jüngeren Bruder Walter
entlassen.

Ich selbst war noch nie ernstlich
krank. Mein Vater starb schon im August
1939. Ich kann mich nicht mehr an ihn er=
innern, da ich damals erst drei Jahre alt
war.

Um einmal meine Mutter unterstützen
zu können, habe ich mir jetzt schon fest
vorgenommen ein tüchtiger (Dreher) zu
werden.

Siegfried Bodenmüller.